Basic Spanish For Police Officers By A Police Officer

by
Jacquelyn MacConnell

authorHOUSE™

1663 LIBERTY DRIVE, SUITE 200
BLOOMINGTON, INDIANA 47403
(800) 839-8640
WWW.AUTHORHOUSE.COM

First published by AuthorHouse 10/05/05

ISBN: 1-4208-9071-9 (sc)

Printed in the United States of America
Bloomington, Indiana

This book is printed on acid-free paper.

DISCLAIMER

The contents of this book are intended as communication aids. The information contained in this book is not intended as tactical advice, nor should it be used counter to the current policies in your law enforcement agency.

ADDITIONAL MATERIALS AVAILABLE

For an accompanying CD to this book and/or laminated cheat sheets that fit into most police cargo and shirt pockets, go to: www.NetCatAZ.com.

ACKNOWLEDGEMENT

Thanks to:

Lennys Toth for helping me put this
project together and narrating the CD.

To Jan Dubina, Mark Geske, Georgia Sevcov, Lisa
Ruggiero and Mariana de la Fuente
for your input and help in editing this book.

Most importantly, to my parents, for their
lifelong support and their
help with this book.

The Phoenix Police Department has graciously
allowed me to reproduce the portion of
this manual that I originally
created for classes
of the Phoenix Police Department's
Post Academy.

TABLE OF CONTENTS

INTRODUCTION

I am a Phoenix Police Sergeant and have worked for the city for twelve years to date (2005). When I was a child, I lived in Colombia, South America and learned Spanish, a language that I had no idea would become so useful later in my life.

In 2000, with the assistance of another officer, I developed a Spanish program for my Department. While some people believe that those living in this country should learn English, my students and I have found it wise to learn a minimal amount of the foreign language spoken in the streets. It is a matter of safety both for the public and the law enforcement professional. As we in law enforcement know, it is often important to control subjects either verbally or with verbal persuasion. One of the languages predominant in the Phoenix metropolitan area is Spanish.

This book does not contain "perfect" Spanish vocabulary. It contains Spanish that will be understood on the street. The Spanish in this book is very basic. It is not meant to make anyone fluent, but rather to permit officers to learn a minimal amount of useful Spanish phrases. I believe this will help officers conduct themselves more safely during their regular duties and achieve the desired result of gaining control and/or information from Spanish speaking subjects. This book contains phrases that will assist you in obtaining basic information for a range of investigations: completing a traffic ticket, traffic accident, assault, domestic violence, stolen vehicle, DUI, burglary, drug investigation and robbery.

However, the most important parts of this book are the High Risk Stop Commands or Command Phrases. Knowing even basic Spanish during these critical moments could save your life, your partner's life, or the life of an innocent bystander.

Learn the Spanish alphabet and how to pronounce each letter. This will enable you to read all the words in this book. When speaking Spanish, if you are not able to speak with a Spanish accent, don't be embarrassed or discouraged. When people from other countries speak English, they speak with an accent. When you speak Spanish, you will, more than likely, have an American accent. This should not concern you. The more you use this language, the more familiar you will become with the words and phrases and that's what is important.

If you see an accent mark over a vowel, it means that the emphasis in that word is placed on that vowel. For example, for the word *atrás*, the emphasis is placed on the second "a".

Again, overall, it is not important if you mispronounce a word. What is important is whether the person you are speaking with understands you. Only concern yourself with the basic grammar listed in this book. When you are more advanced you can learn more vocabulary.

Keep in mind that each Spanish speaking country uses slightly different vocabulary and will have different accents. In comparison, think of American English and an American accent compared to Scottish English and a Scottish accent. Although words and phrases in this book can be used countrywide, the Spanish in this book is based on my experience with subjects living in or visiting the Phoenix metropolitan area.

I have made available a CD that follows this book and will allow you to hear the correct pronunciation of the words. I also have laminated "cheat sheets" available that should fit in your shirt pocket. These contain the high risk stop commands and investigative questions. For more information on these items and/or to order, go to *www.NetCatAZ.com*.

I wish you the best of luck and hope that this book makes your job easier and SAFER.

THE ALPHABET
EL ALFABETO

When you are reading Spanish, you generally pronounce each letter of the word, though there are a very exceptions. It is, therefore, important to know how to pronounce each letter in Spanish. Sometimes the translations sound a lot like their English equivalent. Underneath certain letters are some grammar rules and further explanation of the pronounciation of those letters.

A   (AH)

Abusar	To abuse ("ah boo sahr")
Accidente	Accident ("ax ee den tay")
Acusado	The accused, defendant ("ah coo sah doh")
Arrestar	To arrest ("ah ress tahr")
Apagar	To turn off ("ah pah gahr")

B   (BAY)

Bala	Bullet ("bah lah")
Balazo	Shot, bullet wound ("bah lah so")
Buscar	To look for ("boos kahr")
Barba	Beard ("bahr bah")
Bigote	Mustache ("bee go tay")

"B" and **"V"** SOUND A LOT ALIKE. TO DISTINGUISH BETWEEN THE TWO, YOU CAN ASK A VARIETY OF QUESTIONS, FOR EXAMPLE:

"¿B DE BURRO O V DE VACA?" ("B" FROM THE WORD BURRO OR "V" FROM THE WORD VACA)

OR

"¿B GRANDE O V CHICA?" (THE BIG "B" OR THE LITTLE "V").

1

C (SAY)

Cajuela	Trunk (of a car) ("ka way lah")
Cuadrada	Slang for semi-automatic gun ("kwah drah dah")
¿Cómo?	What? How? ("ko moh")
Carril	Lane (traffic lane) ("kah reel")
Cicatriz	Scar ("see kah treece")

CH   (CHEH)

Choque	Accident (vehicle related) ("cho kay")
Chancla	Slipper, sandal (informal) ("chahn klah")
Chota	Slang for "cop" ("choh tah")

D (DAY)

Detener	To detain ("deh teh nahr")
Delito	Crime ("deh lee toe")
Drogas	Drugs ("droh gahs")
Dinero	Money ("dee nair oh")
Despacio	Slow, slowly ("dehs pah see oh")

E (EH)

Estrangular	To strangle ("ehs strahn goo lahr")
Emergencia	Emergency ("ee mare hen see ah")
Escapar	To escape ("ehs kah pahr")
Escopeta	Shotgun ("es koe peh tah")
Embarazada	Pregnant ("em bah rah sah dah")

F (EFE)

Frenos	Brakes ("fray nose")
Fusca	Slang for firearms ("foos kah")
Feria	Money, cash ("feh ree ah")
Familia	Family ("fah mee lee ah")
Fallecer	To pass away, die ("fah yeh sehr")

G (HAY)

Ganga	Slang for gang ("gahn gah")
Gavacho	White person (may be considered an insult) ("gah vah cho")
Golpear	To hit ("goal pay ahr")
Guante	Glove ("gwan tay")
Güero	Light skinned (same as **huero,** "weh roh")
Gente	People ("hen tay")

"**GU**" FOLLOWED BY AN "I" OR AN "E" = SILENT "U"
   GUITARRA (GUITAR, "gee tahr ah"): "U" IS NOT PRONOUNCED
   GUERRA (WAR, "geh rah"): "U" IS NOT PRONOUNCED

"**GU**" FOLLOWED BY AN "A" OR A CONSONANT, PRONOUNCE ALL LETTERS, FOR EXAMPLE:
   GUTIERREZ (LAST NAME, "goo tee ehr ehz"): HARD "G" SOUND, PRONOUNCE ALL LETTERS
   GUARDAR (TO KEEP, WATCH OVER, "gwahr dahr"): HARD "G" SOUND, PRONOUNCE ALL LETTERS. NORMALLY WITH "GUA" IT MAKES AN ENGLISH "W" SOUND. GUARDAR = "GWARDAR"; **GUAPO** (HANDSOME, "gwah poh") = "GWAPO"

"**G**" FOLLOWED BY AN "E" OR "I", PRONOUNCE THE "G" WITH ENGLISH " H" SOUND. FOR EXAMPLE, **GENTE** IS PRONOUNCED "HEN TAY".

"**G**" FOLLOWED BY AN "A", "O", OR "U", THE "G" MAKES A HARD "G" SOUND. FOR EXAMPLE:
   GATO ("gah toh"), **GOLPEAR** ("gohl peh ahr"), **GUARDAR** ("gwahr dahr").

"*GU*" WITH A DIARISIS OR "GÜ" MAKES A DEFINITIVE "GW" SOUND.
FOR EXAMPLE:

PINGÜINO (PENGUIN) = "PEENG GWEENO"; **BILINGÜE** (BILINGUAL) =
"BEE LING GWAY"

H   (ACHE)

Hambre	Hungry ("ahm bray")
Hijo/hija	Son/daughter ("ee hoe"/"ee hah")
Herido	Wound ("eh ree doh")
Hombre	Man ("ohm bray")
Huero	Light skinned ("weh roh")

"*H*" IS SILENT EXCEPT WHEN WITH "C"; "CH" = CHEH

I   (EE)

Infracción	Infraction (traffic) "een frahk see ohn")
Igual	The same as ("ee gwahl")
Ilegal	Illegal ("ee lay gahl")
Inocente	Innocent ("ee noh sen tay")
Identificar	To identify ("ee dehn tee fee kar")

J   (HOTA)

Jura	Slang for police ("hoo rah")
Juicio	Trial ("hoo ee see oh")
Jueves	Thursday ("hoo ay vays")
Jale	To pull, slang for work ("hah lay")
Juzgar	Adjudicate ("hoos gahr")

"*J*" IN WORDS MAKES AN ENGLISH "H" SOUND, FOR EXAMPLE:
JURA = "HOO RAH"
JALE = "HA LAY"

K   (KAH)

Kilómetro	Kilometer ("kee loh mee troh")
Kilo	Kilogram ("kee low")

L   (ELE)

Lacio	Straight ("lah see oh")
Levantar	To raise, lift ("lay vahn tahr")
Licencia	License ("lee sen see ah")
Lastimar	To hurt, injure ("lahs tee mahr")
Ley	Law ("lay")

"*LL*" TOGETHER MAKES AN ENGLISH "Y" SOUND, FOR EXAMPLE:
LLAVES (KEYS) = "YAH VASE"

M   (EME)

Maltratar	Mistreat ("mahl trah tar")
Maltrato de niños	Child abuse ("mahl trah toe day neen yose")
Multa	Fine, ticket ("mool tah")
Mota	Marijuana (slang) ("moe tah")
Mangas	Sleeves ("mahn gahs")

N   (ENE)

Negro	Black ("nay groh")
Navaja	Knife ("nah vah ha")
Nombre	Name ("nohm bray")
Número	Number ("noo meh roh")
Nieto/nieta	Grandson/granddaughter (nee eh toe/tah")
Nuera	Daughter-in-law ("noo eh rah")

Ñ (ENYE)

Cuñado/cuñada	Brother-in-law/Sister-in-law ("coon yah doh/dah")
Daño	Damage ("dahn yoh")
Años	Years ("ahn yos")
Pañuelo	Handkerchief ("pahn way low")
Piña	Pineapple ("peen yah")

"Ñ" MAKES THE SAME SOUND AS THE LETTER "N" IN THE WORD "CANYON".

"Ñ" VS. **"N"**: PRONOUNCING THE **"Ñ"** WHEN IT IS PRESENT IN A WORD IS VERY IMPORTANT, FOR EXAMPLE:

ANO ("ah noh")	= ANUS
AÑO ("ahn yoh")	= YEAR

O (OH)

Oscuro	Dark ("o skoo roh")
Oficial	Officer, official ("o fee see ahl")
Oro	Gold ("oh row")
Obstruir	To block, obstruct ("ohb stroo ear")
Oído	Ear ("oh ee doh")

P (PAY)

Patrullero/Patrullera	Patrolman, patrolwoman ("pah true yeh roe/pah true yeh rah")
Patrulla	Patrol ("pah true yah")
Patrullar	To patrol ("pah true yahr")
Puño	Fist ("poon yoe")
Placas	License plate, badge ("plah kahs")
Pandilla	Gang ("pahn dee yah")

Q (COO)

Quemadura	Burn ("kay mah doo rah")
Quebrar	To break ("kay brahr")
¿Quién?	Who? ("kee ehn")
Quitar	To remove, take out ("kee tahr")
Querido	Lover, loved one ("kay ree doe")

"QU" ALWAYS HAS AN ENGLISH "K" SOUND, FOR EXAMPLE:
QUEMADURA = "KAY MA DOO RAH"

R (ERE)

Robar	To rob ("row bahr")
Rodillas	Knees ("row dee yahs")
Regresar	To return, to regress ("reh greh sahr")
Rasguño	Scratch ("rahs goon yoh")
Ruca	"Old lady" (slang) ("roo kah")

RR(ERRE)

Carro (car, "kah rroh") vs. **Caro** (expensive, "kah roh")
Perro (dog, "peh rroh") vs. **Pero** (but, "peh roh")

NO WORDS ARE GOING TO START WITH **"RR"**. WHEN THE DOUBLE "R" EXISTS WITHIN A WORD, ROLL THE "R" SOUND.

S (ESAY)

Sangre	Blood ("sahn gray")
Sangrar	To bleed ("sahn grahr")
Secuestrar	To kidnap ("say kwes trahr")
Suéltelo	Drop it ("swell tay low")
Sospechoso	Suspect, suspicious ("sos pay cho soe")

T (TAY)

Tribunal	Court ("tree boo nahl")
Testigo	Witness ("tehs tee go")
Tatuaje	Tattoo ("tah too ah hay")
Temblar	Shiver, tremble ("tehm blahr")
Tampoco	Neither, nor ("tom poe ko")

U (OO)

Uniforme	Uniform ("oo nee for may")
Uña	Nail (fingernail) ("oon yah")
Una	One ("oo nah")
Urgencia	Urgency, urgent need ("oor hen see yah")
Usar	To use ("oo sahr")

V (VAY)

Violación	Sexual assault, rape ("vee oh lah see ohn")
Voltéese	Turn around ("vohl tay eh say")
Vecino	Neighbor ("veh seen oh")
Vecindario	Neighborhood ("ves ehn dah ree oh")
Viejo	Old ("vee a hoe")

"B" and **"V"** SOUND A LOT ALIKE. TO DISTINGUISH BETWEEN THE
TWO, YOU CAN ASK A VARIETY OF QUESTIONS, FOR EXAMPLE:

> **"¿B DE BURRO O V DE VACA?"** ("B" FROM THE WORD BURRO OR "V"
> FROM THE WORD VACA)
>
> OR
>
> **"¿B GRANDE O V CHICA?"** (THE BIG "B" OR THE LITTLE "V").

W (DOBLE OO) OR (DOBLE VAY)

If a word starts with "W", it is normally a borrowed word.
For example, **"whiskey"**.

X (EKEES)	(FEW WORDS START WITH "X")
México/Méjico	Mexico ("Meh hee ko")
Texas/Tejas	Texas ("Tay haas")
Xavier/Javier	Name: Xavier, also spelled Javier ("Ha vee air")
Éxito	Success ("ex ee toe")
Excelente	Excellent ("ex eh lehn tay")

"X" IS OFTEN PRONOUNCED WITH AN ENGLISH "H" SOUND; FOR EXAMPLE:

"**TEXAS**" SPELLED THE SAME IN SPANISH IS PRONOUNCED "TAY HAAS".

HOWEVER, SOMETIMES IT DOES TAKE ON A HARD ENGLISH "X" SOUND, FOR EXAMPLE:

"**ÉXITO**" IS PRONOUNCED "EX EE TOE".

Y (EE GREE A GAH)

Yo	I ("yoh")
Yerno	Son-in-law ("yare noh")

Z (ZETA)

Zapatos	Shoes ("sah pah toes")

"**Z**" OFTEN TAKES ON AN ENGLISH "S" SOUND IN SPANISH, FOR EXAMPLE:

ZAPATOS IS PRONOUNCED "SAH PAH TOES"

MAKE SURE TO DISTINGUISH THE SPELLING OF WORDS THAT ARE COMMONLY SPELLED WITH BOTH A "**Z**" OR AN "**S**", FOR EXAMPLE:*GUTIERREZ/ GUTIERRES*

HERNANDEZ/HERNANDES

RAMIREZ/RAMIRES

DO THIS BY ASKING, *"¿CON ZETA O ESAY?"*

*****SPELLING IS IMPORTANT FOR RECORDING THE SUBJECT'S CORRECT INFORMATION*****

THE VOWELS

A	E	I	O	U
(ah)	(eh)	(ee)	(oh)	(oo)

Pronunciation of the vowels is very important in Spanish and the pronunciation of those vowels does NOT change.

Despacio   ("dehs pah see oh")
Regresar   ("reh greh sahr")
Testigo   ("tehs tee go")

In these examples, the "E" always makes an **"eh"** sound. Each vowel is pronounced as listed above, even when in a word. Look at the word for glove:

Guante   "gwan tay"

If this is broken down further, you can hear the pronunciation of each vowel:
    "Goo ahn tay" OR "Goo ahn teh"

When having a hard time pronouncing a word, break it down after the vowels:

AMETRALLADORA   AH MEH TRAH YAH DOH RAH
NACIONALIDAD   NAH SEE OH NAH LEE DAHD

FALSE COGNATES

WATCH OUT FOR: FALSE COGNATES. WORDS THAT LOOK THE SAME IN ENGLISH AND SPANISH BUT WHICH HAVE DIFFERENT TRANSLATIONS, FOR EXAMPLE:

ÉXITO   MEANS SUCCESS, NOT EXIT
VIOLACIÓN   MEANS SEXUAL ASSAULT, AS WELL AS VIOLATION
                 BUT BE VERY CAREFUL WITH YOUR USE OF THIS
                 WORD, REMEMBERING THAT IT MEANS SEXUAL
                 ASSAULT/RAPE AS WELL
REGISTRAR   MEANS TO SEARCH, AS WELL AS REGISTER

THERE ARE ALSO TRUE COGNATES, FOR EXAMPLE:

REFORMA = REFORM
REGIÓN = REGION
REFORMAR = TO REFORM
HERMAFRODITA = HERMAPHRODITE

THE NUMBERS
LOS NÚMEROS

Cero (0)			
Uno (1)	Once (11)		
Dos (2)	**Doce** (12)	Veinte (20)	**Dos**cientos (200)
Tres (3)	**Tre**ce (13)	**Tre**inta (30)	**Tres**cientos (300)
Cuatro (4)	Catorce (14)	**Cua**renta (40)	**Cuatro**cientos (400)
Cinco (5)	Quince (15)	**Cin**cuenta (50)	Quinientos (500)
Seis (6)	Diecis**éis** (16)	**Se**senta (60)	**Seis**cientos (600)
Siete (7)	Dieci**siete** (17)	**Se**tenta (70)	**Sete**cientos (700)
Ocho (8)	Dieci**ocho** (18)	**Oche**nta (80)	**Ocho**cientos (800)
Nueve (9)	Dieci**nueve** (19)	**No**venta (90)	**Nove**cientos (900)
Diez (10)		Cien (100)	Mil (1000)

For the numbers 16 through 19, the exact translation of the Spanish equivalent is "ten and ....."; for example *dieciséis* exactly translates to "ten and six" (think of it as "*diez y seis*"), or sixteen.

The same translation occurs with "*veinte*" (twenty) through "*noventa*" (ninety); for example, *sesenta y uno* exactly translates to "sixty and one", or sixty-one; *ochenta y uno* exactly translates to "eighty and one", or eighty-one.

WHAT TIME IS IT?
¿QUÉ HORA ES?

When you are talking about one o'clock, it is referred to in the singular (*es*) format, for example:

Es la una	(It is one.)
Ocurió a la una.	(It happened at one.)

The times from two o'clock through twelve o'clock will take on a plural (*son*) format, for example:

Son las dos.	(It is two.)
Son las cinco.	(It is five.)
Son las doce.	(It is twelve.)

Up until 30 minutes after the hour, say the hour and then the minutes, for example:

Son las tres y viente.	*(It is three twenty.)*
Es la una y diecinueve.	(It is one nineteen.)
Son las once y veinticinco.	(It is eleven twenty-five.)
Son las cinco y treinta.	(It is five thirty.)

For the translation of quarter past the hour and half past the hour, the following are commonly used:

Son las cuatro y media.	(It is four thirty.)
Son las siete y cuarto.	(It is seven and a quarter OR It is seven fifteen.)

For thirty through fifty-nine past the hour, the common translations are:

Son las cinco menos once.
(Four forty-nine OR It is five minus eleven.)

Son las ocho menos vienticinco.
(Seven thirty-five OR It is eight minus twenty-five.)

Son las diez menos quince OR ***Son las diez menos cuarto.***
(Nine forty-five OR It is ten minus a quarter.)

Son las once para las cinco.
(It is eleven until five. OR Four forty-nine.)

Son las veinticinco para las ocho.
(It is twenty-five until eight. OR Seven thirty-five.)

Son las quince para las diez.
(It is fifteen until ten. OR Nine forty-five.)

When talking about morning or night, the following are commonly used:

Son las dos en la mañana. OR ***Son las dos de la mañana.***
(It is two in the morning.)

Son las dos en la tarde. OR ***Son las dos de la tarde.***
(It is two in the afternoon.)

Son las once en la noche. OR ***Son las once de la noche.***
(It is eleven at night.)

MONTHS OF THE YEAR
MESES DEL AÑO

Enero	(January)
Febrero	(February)
Marzo	(March)
Abril	(April)
Mayo	(May)
Junio	(June)
Julio	(July)
Agosto	(August)
Septiembre	(September)
Octubre	(October)
Noviembre	(November)
Diciembre	(December)

All of the months except January, have essentially the same base part of the word in Spanish as they do in English; for example "*Mayo*" is May, "*Marzo*" is March, "*Septiembre*" sounds like September.

DAYS OF THE WEEK
DÍAS DE LA SEMANA

lunes	Monday	From the word "Lunar"
martes	Tuesday	From the planet "Mars"
miércoles	Wednesday	From the planet "Mercury"
jueves	Thursday	From the planet "Jupiter"
viernes	Friday	From the planet "Venus"
sábado	Saturday	From the word "Sabbath"
domingo	Sunday	From the word "Domini" or lord

Days of the week are NOT capitalized in Spanish.

Ways of referring to different days of the week:

El próximo, la próxima = the next (*el próximo sábado* = the next Saturday; *la próxima mañana*)

(DO NOT OVERLY CONCERN YOURSELF WITH "*EL*" AND "*LA*" {both mean "the"}. YOU WILL BE UNDERSTOOD REGARDLESS.)

Mañana = tomorrow

Ayer = yesterday

Antes de ayer = literally "before yesterday" OR the day before Yesterday (In Mexico, will hear it as "*antier*")

Pasado mañana = literally "past tomorrow" OR the day after tomorrow

Este = this (*este jueves* = this Thursday)

En la mañana = in the morning

Por la mañana = in the morning

Esta mañana = this morning

Que viene = this coming (*el lunes que viene* = the upcoming Monday, or literally "the Monday that is coming")

Pasado = past (*el domingo pasado* = the past Sunday)

Anoche = last night

COLORS
COLORES

Blanco	(White)
Negro	(Black)
Azul	(Blue)
Morado	(Purple)
Plomo	(Dark gray, lead gray)
Dorado	(Gold)
Plateado	(Silver)
Cobre/Cobrigo	(Copper)
Amarillo	(Yellow)
Verde	(Green)
Rojo	(Red)
Guinda	(Dark Red/Burgundy)
Rosa	(Pink)
Anaranjado/Naranja	(Orange)
Café/Marrón	(Brown)
Gris	(Gray)
Azul marino	(Navy blue)
Celeste	(Light blue)
Violeta	(Violet)

WEEPONS
ARMAS

¿Tenía armas? ¿Qué tipo?   (Did they have weapons? What kind?)

Cuchillo	(Knife)
Fila	(Knife – slang)
Filero	(Knife – slang)
Navaja	(Knife, specifically pocket knife)
Pistola	(Pistol)
Cuete	(Gun – slang, literally "firecracker")
Fusca	(Gun – slang)
Cuadrada	Semi-automatic – slang)
Automático/a	(Automatic)
Cromo/Cromada	(Chrome)
Plateado/a	(Silver)
Negro/a	(Black)
Escopeta	(Shotgun)
Ametralladora	(Machine gun)
Metralleta	
Rifle/Fusil	(Rifle)
Subfusil	(Sub machine gun)
Cuerno de chivo	(AK-47 – slang, literally means *"horns of the goat"*)
Cuerno	(AK-47 – slang, literally "horns")
Chivo	(AK-47 – slang, literally "goat")
Palo	(Stick)
Ladrillo	(Brick)
Pipa	(Pipe)
Bate	(Bat)

MISCELLANEOUS EXPRESSIONS

Mátalo/Mátala	*(Kill him/Kill her)*	**Matar** = to kill
Pícalo/Pícala	*(Stab him/stab her)*	**Picar** = to stab
Dale un chinganazo/		= punch him/her (slang)
un pegazo		
Agárralo/Agárrala	*(Grab him/grab her)*	**Agarrar** = to grab
Ponte trucha		= be careful, be watchful
Ponte agua		= be aware
Chota		= "cops" (slang)
Jura		= "cops" (slang)
Placa		= badge; slang for police
Perros		= dogs; slang for police
Chueco		= crooked; often used in terms of driver's license/identifications, ie. fake identification

INJURIES OR MEANS OF AN ATTACK
HERIDAS

Heridas	= injuries
Moretón	= bruise
Raspadura	= scrape; "rasberry"
Arañazo	= scratch
Rasguño	= scratch
Quebrado/a	= broken
Dolor	= pain
Cachetada	= slap
Pata/Patada	=kick/kicked
Puño/Puñazo/Puñetazo	= punch
Puñalada	= stabbing

FRIENDS AND FAMILY MEMBERS
AMIGOS Y MIEMBROS DE LA FAMILIA

Amigo/amiga	= friend (male/female)
Pariente	= relative
Esposo/esposa	= husband/wife
Hermano/hermana	= brother/sister
Hijo/hija	=son/daughter
Padre	= father
Madre	= mother
Novio/novia	= boyfriend/girlfriend
Abuelo/abuela	= grandfather/grandmother
Nieto/nieta	= grandson/granddaughter
Ahijado/Ahijada	= God son/God daughter
Primo/prima	= cousin (male/female)
Tío/tía	= uncle/aunt
Sobrino/sobrina	= nephew/niece
Cuñado/cuñada	= brother-in-law/sister-in-law
Suegro/suegra	= father-in-law/mother-in-law
Yerno/Nuera	= son-in-law/daughter-in-law

BODY PARTS
PARTES DEL CUERPO

Brazo(s)	= arm(s)
Pierna(s)	= leg(s)
Espalda	= back
Ojos	= eyes
Cejas	= eyebrows
Pecho	= Chest
Codo	= Elbow
Rodillas	= knees
Boca	= mouth
Dientes	= teeth
Cabeza	= head
Dedos	= fingers
Pies	= feet
Dedos del pie	= toes
Hombros	= shoulders
Manos	= hands

PARTS OF A VEHICLE
PARTES DE UN VEHÍCULO

Motor	= motor
Asiento	= seat
Tablero del carro	= dashboard
Cajuela	= trunk
Cofre	= hood
Luces del frente/Luces delanteras	= headlights
Luces traseras	= tail lights
Luces de frenos	= brake lights
Luces de giro/direccional	= turning lights
Defensa	= bumper
Guardafango	= fender
Llanta	= tire
Volante	= steering wheel

COMMON JOBS AND LOCATIONS
TRABAJOS CORRIENTE Y LUGARES

Las yardas/"landscaping"	= yard work/landscaping
Jardinero	= gardener
Los techos	= works on roofs
Construccíon	= construction
Cajera	= cashier
Carnicero	= butcher
Carnicería	= meat store
Panadero	= baker
Panadería	= bakery
Mecánico	= mechanic
Restaurante	= restaurant
Mesero/a	= waiter/waitress
Tienda	= store (small)
Mercado	= store
Empleado	= employee

HELPFUL WORDS TO USE WHEN TALKING TO SPANISH SPEAKING SUBJECTS

Despacio   = slow, slowly

   For example: ***Habla despacio por favor.*** = Talk slowly please.

Repita por favor   = repeat please

¿Cómo se escribe?   = How do you spell it?

Hablo poco español.   = I speak a little Spanish.

Un número a la vez.   = one number at a time

   For example: ***Su seguro social, un número a la vez.***

      = Your social security number, one number at a time.

Enséñeme   = show me
Enséñeme dónde   = show me where
No entiendo.   = I do not understand.
Dígame sí o no.   = Tell me yes or no.

HIGH RISK STOP COMMANDS AND/OR HIGH RISK COMMANDS

The next three sections, General Vocabulary, Related to the Car and Verbs, contain words that will be used in the "High Risk Stop Commands" or the "Command Phrases". If you can learn these words prior learning the command phrases, you will be able to say the phrases much more easily.

General Vocabulary

Por favor	*(Please)*
Levántese	*(Stand up)*
Siéntese	*(Sit down)*
Rodilla	*(Knee)*
Cara	*(Face)*
Cabeza	*(Head)*
Manos	*(Hands)*
Pies	*(Feet)*
Boca	*(Mouth)*
Paso	*(Step)*
Espalda	*(Back)*
A su izquierda	*(To your left)*
A su derecha	*(To your right)*
Derecho	*(Straight)*
Arma	*(Weapon)*
Policía de (your city)	*(…….. Police)*
Todos	*(Everyone)*
Afuera	*(Out, outside)*
Suelo	*(Ground)*
Silencio	*(Silence)*
No hablen.	*(Do not talk)*
Cállese.	*(Shut up)*
Despacio	*(Slow, slowly)*

Related to the Car

Conductor	(Driver)
Pasajero	(Passenger)
De atrás	(Of the back)
Del frente	(Of the front)
Puerta	(Door)
Llaves	(Keys)
Carro	(Car)
Ventana	(Window)
Motor	(Motor)

The Verbs

Mueva	(Move – singular, command)
Apague	(Turn off – singular, command)
Tire	(Throw – singular, command)
Ponga	(Put – singular, command)
Abra	(Open – singular command)
Salga	(Get out – singular, command)
Regrese	(Regress, return – singular, command)
Voltéese	(Turn around – singular, command)
Levante	(Lift – singular, command)
Camine	(Walk – singular, command)
Alto	(Stop – command)
Separe	(Separate – singular, command)
Cruce	(Cross – singular, command)
Suéltelo	(Drop it – command)
Cálmese	(Calm down – singular, command)
Silencio	(Silence, quiet)
Acuéstese	(Lay down – command)
Tírese	(Throw – command)

Command Phrases – Putting the Vocabulary Together

¡Todos, manos arriba! OR
¡Todos, manos en la cabeza!
(Everyone, hands up! OR Everyone, hands on your head!)

¡No se muevan!
(Do not move!)

¡Conductor, apague el motor!
(Driver, turn off the motor!)

Tire las llaves afuera de la ventana. OR *Ponga las llaves afuera de la ventana y suéltelas.* OR *Llaves afuera. Suéltelas.*
(Throw the keys out the window. OR Put the keys out the window and drop them. OR Keys out. Drop them.)

Conductor, abra la puerta.
(Driver, open the door.)

Conductor, salga del carro. OR *Conductor, bájese del carro.*
(Driver, get out of the car.)

Conductor, regrese al carro.
(Driver, return to the car. OR Driver, get back in the car.)

¡Manos arriba!
(Hands up!)

¡Voltéese!
(Turn around!)

Levante la camisa.
(Lift your shirt.)

Abra la chaqueta.
(Open your jacket.)

Camine para atrás (hacia mí).
(Walk backwards {towards me}.)

¡Alto!
(Stop!)

Un paso a su derecha/izquierda.
(One step to your right/left.)

Acuéstese, boca abajo OR Tírese al suelo.
(Lay down, mouth down OR Throw yourself onto the ground.)

De rodillas. Cruce los pies.
(On your knees. Cross your feet.)

Separe los pies. Manos en la espalda/la cabeza.
(Separate your feet. Hands on your back/head.)

Está arrestado.
(You are arrested.)

Pasajero del frente....
(Front passenger)

REPEAT COMMANDS TO TAKE FRONT PASSENGER(S) INTO CUSTODY

Pasajero de atrás ....
(Back passenger)

Lado izquierdo OR Lado derecho
(Left side OR Right side)

Un pasajero de atrás

(One back passenger.)

REPEAT COMMANDS TO TAKE BACK SEAT PASSENGER(S) INTO CUSTODY

Additional Commands and Vocabulary

Veo el arma. ¡No la toque!

(I see the weapon. Do not touch it.)

Ponga el arma en el suelo.

(Put the weapon on the floor.)

¡Suéltela!

(Drop it!)

Más.

(More)

Míreme.

(Look at me.)

No me mire.

(Don't look at me.)

No se mueva.

(Do not move.)

No hablen. OR No hable.

(Do not talk – plural and singular.)

For the command phrases listed above, you can mix the phrases up for your own purposes, depending on who you are contacting.

For a **high risk stop**, when you are taking the back passengers out of the car, you can either identify which passenger by saying:

Pasajero de atrás, lado derecho, ¡salga del carro!

(Back passenger, right side, get out of the car!)

OR

You can just say "one back passenger" and then complete the commands:

Un pasajero de atrás, ¡salga del carro!

(One back passenger, get out of the car!)

Example of a High Risk Contact:

¡Policía de ....!

¡Alto!

¡Levante la camisa! Despacio.

¡Volteése! Despacio.

¡Alto! (Tell them this when facing away from you.)

¡De rodillas!

¡Manos en la cabeza!

Está arrestado.

(You just identified yourself, had someone stop, lift their shirt slowly, turn around, stop facing away from you, get on their knees, put their hands on their head, and then told them they were under arrest.)

The above phrases also give you the vocabulary to take someone into custody...

Standing up:	**Camine atrás.**
	¡Alto!
	¡Separe los pies!
	¡Manos en la cabeza!
Kneeling:	**Camine atrás.**
	¡Alto!
	¡De rodillas!
	¡Manos en la cabeza!
	¡Cruce los pies!
	¡No se mueva!

Laying down: *Camine atrás.*
                         ¡Alto!
                         ¡No me mire!
                         ¡No hable!
                         ¡De rodillas!
                         ¡Tírese al suelo!
                         ¡Manos en la cabeza!
                         ¡Cruce los pies!

Some of the commands allow several phrases that mean the same thing. Choose the phrase that is easier for you to pronounce and memorize. For example: *"Tírese al suelo"* AND *"Acuéstese boca abajo"* mean essentially the same thing. Which one is easier for you to pronounce? Both are idiomatic expressions and do not make a lot of sense when translated literally, but both phrases are telling someone to lay on the ground, face down.

Also, remember, you do NOT have to memorize each command listed above to conduct a high risk traffic stop or high risk contact. By learning or memorizing just a few phrases, you will be able to conduct a high risk stop or contact in Spanish more safely than if you knew nothing.

For example:

¡Todos manos arriba!	(Everyone, hands up!)
¡Silencio!	(Silence!)
¡Conductor salga!	(Driver, get out!)
¡Camine para atrás!	(Walk backwards!)
¡Alto!	(Alto!)
¡Manos en la cabeza!	(Hands on your head!)
¡Un pasajero salga!	(One passenger, get out!)
¡Camine para atrás!	(Walk backwards!)
¡Alto!	(Stop!)
¡Manos en la cabeza!	(Hands on your head!)

By learning those ten commands, you should be able to take both the front and back passengers out of the car safely.

INVESTIGATIONS
INVESTIGACIÓNES

Obtaining a Person's Personal Information

¿Cómo se llama, nombre completo?
(What is your name, complete name?)

Nombre, apellido paterno, apellido materno
(Name, paternal last name, maternal last name)

¿Cómo se escribe?
(How do you spell it?)

Repita por favor OR Otra vez, despacio.
(Repeat it please OR again, slowly.)

¿Cuándo nació? ¿Fecha de nacimiento?
(When were you born? Date of birth?)

Mes, día, año
(Month, day, year)

Un número a la vez.
(One number at a time.)

¿Su seguro social?
(Your social security number?)

Un número a la vez.
(One number at a time.)

¿Su dirección exacta? (del domicilio)
(Your exact address. …of your house.)

Este
(East)

Oeste
(West)

Norte
(North)

Sur
(South)

Calle
(Street)

Avenida
(Avenue)

¿Apartamento o casa?
(Apartment or house?)

¿Ciudad y estado?
(City and State)

¿Código postal?
(Zip code)

¿Número de teléfono? (¿el areá?)
(Telephone number? ....the area code?)

¿Dónde trabaja?
(Where do you work?)

¿Nombre de su empleo?
(Name of your employer?)

¿La dirección?
(The address?)

¿Número de teléfono?
(Telephone number?)

¿Cuánto mide? (en pies y pulgadas)
(How tall are you? ....in feet and inches.)

¿Cuánto pesa? (en libras)
(How much do you weigh? ....in pounds.)

General Information Relating to Obtaining Personal Information

NAMES: Most Latin cultures use both their maternal and paternal last names along with their first names, often times not having what we refer to as a "middle name". For example:

Luis Carlos **_Lopez_** **_Rodriguez_**
(First name) (Paternal) (Maternal)

Ana Teresa **_Manzo_** **_de Castillo_**
(First name) (Paternal) (Husband's last name)

For this reason, when you ask for a last name, specify whether you are asking for their paternal last name, maternal last name, or both. Often times, if you ask for a middle name, they will tell you they do not have one. For these reasons, at a minimum, ask for their COMPLETE NAME.

When **_Luis Carlos Lopez Rodriguez_** becomes Americanized, he will most likely go by **_Luis Lopez_**. When **_Ana Teresa Manzo de Castillo_** becomes Americanized, she will mostly likely go by **_Ana Castillo_**.

If they provide you with a foreign identification, confirm which name is their paternal and which is their maternal last name. Make sure you make note of all of the different parts of their name as it is important for our respective criminal history/contact systems (NCIC). If it does not all fit on your form, list the others as AKA's in the hopes that other officers will be able to locate their information in the future. Remember, this information is not only for you. If this is the first time this person will be entered into the system, this information is for each officer who comes into contact with this person in the future. **DO IT RIGHT!**

DATE OF BIRTH: When asking for a date of birth, most Latin cultures will give the day, the month, and then the year. Also, it is possible for someone not to know their date of birth. Although we find this very hard to understand, if you are dealing with someone of a lower socio-economic status, their date of birth may be irrelevant to them. This is not always the case, but keep it in mind.

HEIGHT AND WEIGHT: When asking for height and weight, remember, they do not use feet and pounds so they may not be able to give you the numbers you are asking for. They use the metric system. They will use meters and kilograms, 1 kilogram = 2.2 pounds and 0.3 meters = 1 foot. For example, 5 feet 5 inches = 1.65 meters.

If you are given kilograms and meters, estimate. If they give you the answer in feet/inches and pounds, they most likely did not just arrive and have some knowledge of our culture and understanding of our language.

PHYSICAL ADDRESSES: Regarding addresses, in some Latin American countries they do not use zip codes; for this reason, remembering zip codes is often difficult. Again, if dealing with someone from a lower socio-economic background, their address may never have been important in the past and they may not know their exact current address. It is not uncommon, however, for them to be able to describe exactly where they live and give you an apartment number.

NICKNAMES: In most Latin American cultures, nicknames are very common. It is not unusual for someone to know an acquaintance by only their nickname.

Obtaining a Suspect's Personal Information

¿Conoce al sospechoso? **IF YES:**
(Do you know the suspect?)

¿Sabe el nombre? ¿Sí o no?
(Do you know his/her name? Yes or no?)

Information on a known suspect:

¿Cómo se llama él/ella, nombre completo?
(What is his/her name, complete name?)

Nombre, apellido paterno, apellido materno
(Name, paternal last name, maternal last name?)

¿Tiene apodo/sobrenombre?
(Does he/she have a nickname?)

¿Cuántos años tiene?
(How old is he/she?)

¿Sabe cuándo nació él/ella? ¿Fecha de nacimiento?
(Do you know when he/she was born? Date of birth?)

Mes, día, año
(Month, day, year)

¿Sabe el seguro social de él/ella?
(Do you know his/her social security number?)

¿Sabe dónde vive él/ella? (el domicilio)
(Do you know where he/she lives? …their house.)

¿La direccíon exacta?
(The exact address?)

¿Sabe el número de teléfono de él/ella?

(Do you know his/her telephone number?)

¿Sabe dónde trabaja él/ella?

(Do you know where he/she works?)

¿Nombre del empleo?

(Name of employer? {Refers to an organization})

¿Nombre de su jefe?

(Name of your boss?)

¿La dirección?

(The address?)

¿Número de teléfono?

(Telephone number?)

IF SUSPECT IS UNKNOWN: (see suspect physical description on next page.)

SUSPECT PHYSICAL DESCRIPTION, WHETHER KNOWN OR UNKNOWN:

¿La nacionalidad del sospechoso?	(The suspect's nationality?)
Mexicano/Latino	(Mexican/Latin)
Americano	(American)
Chicano/Pocho	(Mexican-American, usually does not speak Spanish well)
Negro/Moreno/Prieto	(Black/dark skin)
Chino/Asiático	(Chinese/Asian)
¿El edad del sospechoso? OR	(The age of the suspect? OR
¿Cuantos años tiene el sospechoso?	How old is the suspect?)
Más o menos	(more or less)
Viejo	(old)
Joven	(young)
¿El sospechoso/a era:	(The suspect was:....)
Flaco	(Skinny)
Delgado	(Thin)
Mediano	(Medium)
Gordo/Panzón	(Fat)
Musculoso	(Muscular)
¿Cuánto pesa? (en libras)	(How much did he/she weigh? ...in pounds)
¿Cuánto mide? (en pies y pulgadas)	(How tall was he/she? ....in feet and inches.)
Alto	(Tall)
Bajo	(Short)
Chaparro	(Little)

Can use the word **"igual"** (*the same as*) to assist with getting descriptions.

For example: ***Igual que yo*** (*the same as me.*)

Igual que el/ella. (*The same as him/her.*)

Hair color:	**¿Pelo rubio?**	(Blonde hair?)
	¿Pelo café/castaño?	(Brown hair?)
	¿Pelo negro?	(Black hair?)
	¿Pelo rojo/pelirojo?	(Red hair?)
	¿Pelo gris?	(Gray hair?)
Hair length:	**¿Pelo largo?**	(Long hair?)
	¿Pelo corto?	(Short hair?)
Hair style:	**¿Pelo lacio?**	(Straight hair?)
	¿Pelo rizado?	(Curly hair?)
	¿Pelón?	(Bald?)
	¿Pelo chino?	(Curly hair? May be construed as straight, so verify with "lacio o rizado")
	¿Tenía trenzas?	(Did he/she have braids?)
	¿Tenía cola/cola de caballo?	(Did he/she have a pony tail?)
Facial hair:	**¿Tenía barba?**	(Did he have a beard?)
	¿Tenía bigote?	(Did he have a mustache?)
	¿Estaba bien afeitado?	(Was he well shaven?)
	¿Tenía patillas?	(Did he have side burns?)
	¿Tenía chivo/candado?	(Did he have a goatee?)

Speech characteristics:	**¿Tenía acento?**	(Did he/she have an accent?)
	¿Tenía voz alta?	(Did he/she have a loud voice?)
	¿Tenía voz baja?	(Did he/she have a quiet voice?)
	¿Tenía mala pronunciación?	(Did he/she have bad pronounciation?)
	¿Tenía voz normal?	(Did he/she have a normal voice?)
	¿Habló ingles o español?	(Did he/she speak English or Spanish?)

Complexion:	¿Piel clara? (huero/güero)	(Light skinned?)
	¿Piel oscura?	(Dark skinned?)
	¿Tenía pecas?	(Did he/she have freckles?)
	¿Tenía acné?	(Did he/she have acne?)

Eyes:	¿Ojos azules?	(Blue eyes?)
	¿Ojos verdes?	(Green eyes?)
	¿Ojos cafés?	(Brown eyes?)
	¿Ojos negros?	(Black eyes?)
	¿Ojos grandes?	(Big eyes?)
	¿Ojos pequeños?	(Little eyes?)

Identifying features:

Tattoos:

¿Tenía tatuaje? If yes:

(Did he/she have a tattoo?)

de letras?	(of letters?)
de números?	(of numbers?)
de un símbolo?	(of a symbol?)
de un animal?	(of an animal?)
de un dibujo o foto?	(of a picture?)
de puntos? (los tres puntos)	(of dots?
	The three dots?)

Say "Enséñeme dónde"   (Show me where.)

***Have them show you where the tattoo is.

¿Tenía otro tatuaje?   (Did he/she have another tattoo?)

Scars:

¿Tenía cicatriz?   (Did he/she have a scar?)

If yes: Enséñeme dónde.

Moles:

¿Tenía lunares?   (Did he/she have moles?)

****Use "enséñeme dónde" whenever wanting them to
show you where something is.****

CLOTHING
LA ROPA

Men and Women's Clothing: *¿Tenía*.... (Did he/she have....?)

Camiseta	(T-shirt)
T-shirt (slang)	
Camisa	(Shirt)
Pulóver	(Pull-over)
Blusa	(Blouse)
Pantalones	(Pants)
De mezclilla	(Jeans)
Pantalones cortos	(Shorts)
Chorts (slang)	
Falda	(Skirt)
Vestido	(Dress)
Cinturón/cinto	(Belt)
Hebilla	(Belt buckle)
Calcetines	(Socks)

Jackets: *¿Tenía* (Did he/she have......?)

Abrigo	(Heavy coat)
Chaqueta	(Jacket)
Playera	(Light jacket, work out jacket)
Chamarra	(Light jacket)
Chaleco	(Vest)

Miscellaneous reference clothing:

¿Tenía mangas largas?	(Did he/she have long sleeves?)
¿Tenía mangas cortas?	(Did he/she have short sleeves?)
Rayada	(Stripes)
Cuadrada/A cuadros	(Plaid)
Estampada	(Design)
¿Tenía bolsillos/bolsas?	(Did he/she have pockets?)
Con	(With)
Sin	(Without)

Shoes: *¿Tenía......*   (Did he/she have......?)

   Zapatos   (Shoes)

   Botas   (Boots)

   Zapatos de tenis   (Tennis shoes)

   Chanclas/chancletas/   (Sandals)
   guaraches/sandalias

   Tacones altos.   (High heels)

Hats: *¿Tenía......*   (Did he/she have.....?)

   Sombrero   (Cowboy hat)

   Gorra/cachucha   (Baseball hat)

   Pañuelo   (Handkerchief)

   ¿Con letras o marcas?   (With letters or marks?)

Accessories:

   ¿Tenía joyas?   (Did he/she have jewelry?)

   ¿De oro?   (Of gold?)

   ¿De plata?   (Of silver?)

   ¿Tenía aretes?   (Did he/she have earrings?)

   ¿Tenía collar/cadena? (Did he/she have a necklace?)

   ¿Tenía pulsera/brazalete? (Did he/she have a bracelet?)

   ¿Tenía seminario?   (Did he/she have a bracelet?)
                                {several bracelets worn
                                together}

   ¿Tenía anillo?   (Did he/she have a ring?)

   ¿Tenía reloj?   (Did he/she have a watch?)

   ¿Tenía anteojos/lentes/gafas? (Did he/she have glasses?)

   ¿Tenía anteojos del sol/lentes del sol? (Did he/she have sun glasses)

Example: *¿Tenía camisa?*

     IF YES: *¿Con mangas largas o cortas?*
                   ¿Color azul, verde, rojo?

     IF NO: *¿Tenía pulóver, camiseta?*
                   ¿Tenía abrigo, chaqueta o playera?
                   ¿Tenía joyas?

     IF YES: *¿De oro? ¿De plata?*
                   ¿Tenía reloj?

VEHICLE INFORMATION
INFORMACIÓN DE EL VEHÍCULO

¿Tenían un vehículo?	(Did they have a vehicle?)
¿Qué tipo?	(What kind?)
Carro	(Car)
Camioneta	(Van)
Van (slang)	
Camión o Camioneta	(Truck)
Troka (slang)	
Doble cabina	(Double cabin, extended cab)
¿El año?	(The year?)
¿Nuevo o viejo?	(New or old?)

Size
Pequeño	(Little/small)
Grande	(Big)
¿Qué clase? ¿Honda, Chevy, Ford?	(What make?)
¿Bien o mal pintado?	(Good or badly painted?)
¿Oxidedo?	(Rusty?)
¿Con calcomanías?	(With stickers?)
¿Dos o cuatro puertas?	(Two or four doors?)
¿Número/letras de la placa?	(Numbers/letters of the license plate?)
¿Estado?	(State)
¿Qué color era?	(What color was it?)
¿Estaba dañado?	(Was it damaged?)
Enséñeme dónde.	(Show me where.)

TRAFFIC STOPS

General Vocabulary

Señora	(Mrs.)
Señorita	(Ms.)
Señor	(Mr.)
Por favor	(Please)
Licencia o identificación	(License or identification.)
Registro (matrícula)	(Registration)
Seguro del carro (aseguranza)	(Car insurance)
Infracción de tráfico	(Traffic infraction)
Multa (slang: tickete)	(Ticket/fine)
¿Correcto?	(Correct?)

Obtaining Information

¿Tiene licencia o identificación?
(Do you have a license or identification?)

¿de Arizona?
(from Arizona?)

¿de México?
(from Mexico?)

Quiero verlo por favor.
(I would like to see it please.)

¿Tiene seguro del carro?
(Do you have car insurance?)

¿Tiene registro del carro? (slang: *registracíon*)
(Do you have the car registration?)

Obtaining Personal Information

¿Cómo se llama, nombre completo?
(What is your name, your complete name?)

Nombre, apellido paterno, apellido materno
(First name, paternal last name, maternal last name)

¿Cuándo nació? OR ¿Fecha de nacimiento?
(When were you born? OR Your date of birth?)

Mes, día, año
(Month, day, year)

¿Su seguro social?
(Your social security number?)

¿Su dirección exacta? (del domicilio)
(Your exact address?   ....of your house.)

¿Código postal?
(Zip code?)

¿Número de teléfono?
(Telephone number?)

¿Dónde trabaja?
(Where do you work?)

¿Nombre de su empleo?
(Name of your employer?)   **OR**

¿Nombre del negocio dónde trabaja?
(Name of the business where you work.)

¿La dirección?
(The address?)

¿Número de teléfono?
(Telephone number?)

¿Cuánto mide? (en pies y pulgadas.)
(How tall are you? …in feet and inches.)

¿Cuánto pesa? (en libras)
(How much do you weigh? …..in pounds.)

Miscellaneous

¿Ha sido arrestado antes en Arizona?
(Have you been arrested before in Arizona?)

¿Cuándo?
(When?)

¿Qué nombre usó?
(What name did you use?)

Salga del carro, por favor.
(Get out of the car, please.)

Está arrestado.
(You are arrested/under arrest.)

¿Puedo registrar su carro?
(Can I search your car?)

Firme aquí.
(Sign here.)

Puede pagar la multa o puede ir a corte en este día.

(You can pay the ticket/fine or you can go to court on this day.)

ASSAULT – DOMESTIC VIOLENCE

The following questions will allow you to obtain enough information to take a very basic assault report and to determine whether it is domestic violence related. It will further allow you to ascertain specific details if it is domestic violence.

To obtain the victim's personal information, refer to "Obtaining A Person's Personal Information" on page 34 of this book. When you reach the point of obtaining the suspect's personal information (known or unknown suspect) refer to page 41.

The following questions are asked in a "tu" form instead of "usted" (less formal) in an attempt to have a more familiar or friendly tone with the victim. The questions are specifically related to an assault:

¿Quién te pegó?   **OR**   *¿Alguien te pegó?*

(Who hit you?)   **OR**   (Did someone hit you?)

¿Quién era?

(Who was it?)

DOMESTIC VIOLENCE RELATED:

¿Es pariente?   (Is he/she family?)

    Esposo/Esposa   (Husband/Wife)

    Ex-esposo/Ex-esposa   (Ex-husband/Ex-wife)

    Hijo/Hija   (Son/Daughter)

(REFER TO PAGE 22 FOR MORE FAMILY WORDS & TRANSLATIONS)

CURRENTLY MARRIED:

¿Están casados?

(Are you married?)

¿Por cuánto tiempo han estado casados?

(How long have you been married?)

¿Quién vive aquí?

(Who lives here?)

PREVIOUSLY MARRIED:

¿Estaban casados?
(Were you married?)

¿Por cuánto tiempo estaban casados?
(How long were you married?)

¿Por cuánto tiempo han estado divorciados?
(How long have you been divorced?)

NOT MARRIED BUT LIVING TOGETHER:

¿Viven juntos?
(Do you live together?)

¿Por cuánto tiempo han vivido juntos?
(How long have you lived together?)

LIVED TOGETHER IN THE PAST

¿Vivían juntos?
(Did you live together?)

¿Por cuánto tiempo han vivido juntos?
(How long did you live together?)

¿Por cuánto tiempo viven separados?
(How long have you lived separately?)

CHILDREN IN COMMON

¿Está embarazada?
(Are you pregnant?)

¿Tienen niños juntos?
(Do you have children together?)
¿Cuántos?
(How many?)

¿Cuántos años tienen los niños?
(How old are the children?)
OR
¿Cuántos años tiene su niño/niña?
(How old is your son/daughter?)

THE ASSAULT

¿Cómo te pegó?
(How did he/she hit you?)

¿Con mano abierta o cerrada?
(With an open hand or a closed hand?)

¿Cuántos veces te pegó?
(How many times did he/she hit you?)

¿Dónde te pegó?   Enséñame.
(Where did he/she hit you? Show me.)

¿Tiene heridas?
(Do you have injuries?)

¿Tiene moretones?
(Do you have bruises?)

¿Tiene marcas?
(Do you have marks?)

¿Tiene dolor?
(Are you in pain? Or Do you have pain?)

    ¿Dónde?
    (Where?)

¿Necesita atención medíca?
(Do you need medical attention?)

¿Usó un arma?
(Did he/she use a weapon?)

¿Qué tipo?
(What type?)

¿Hay testigos?
(Are there witnesses?)

    ¿Quién?
    (Who?)

REFER TO PAGE 19 FOR WEAPONS

BURGLARY INVESTIGATION

The following questions will allow you to obtain enough information to take a very basic burglary report.

To obtain the victim's personal information, refer to "Obtaining A Person's Personal Information" on page 34 of this book. When you reach the point of obtaining the suspect's personal information (known or unknown suspect) refer to page 41.

The following questions are specifically related to a burglary:

¿A qué hora salió de la casa?

(What time did you leave the house?)

¿A qué hora regresó?

(What time did you return?)

¿Cómo entró el sospechoso?

(How did the suspect get in?)

¿Qué le falta?

(What are you missing?)

¿Tiene idea de quién es el sospechoso?

(Do you have an idea who the suspect is?)

      IF YES:

      ¿Quién?

      (Who?)

(GO TO PAGE 39 TO OBTAIN A SUSPECT'S INFORMATION)

¿Hay testigos?

(Are there witnesses?)

¿Quién?

(Who?)

ROBBERY INVESTIGATION

The following questions will allow you to obtain enough information to take a very basic robbery report.

To obtain the victim's personal information, refer to "Obtaining A Person's Personal Information" on page 34 of this book. When you reach the point of obtaining the suspect's personal information (known or unknown suspect) refer to page 41.

The following questions are specifically related to a robbery.

¿Qué han robado?
(What was stolen?)

¿Tenían armas?
(Did they have weapons?)
> **¿Qué tipo?**
> (What type?)
> **OR** refer to page 19

¿Conoce al sospechoso/los sospechosos, sí o no?
(Do you know the suspect/s, yes or no?)

(GO TO PAGE 39 FOR OBTAINING A SUSPECT'S INFORMATION)

¿Más o menos, a que hora ocurrió?
(More or less, at what time did this occur?)

¿Dónde ocurrió?
(Where did it occur?)
> POSSIBLY USE: **Enséñame donde.**

¿Hay testigos?
(Were there witnesses?)

¿Tiene heridas?
(Do you have injuries?)

¿Quiere denunciarlo?

(Do you want to prosecute/report him?)

   OR

¿Quiere ir a la corte para testificar contra el sospechoso/los sospechosos?

(Do you want to go to court to testify against the suspect/s?)

ACCIDENT INVESTIGATION

The following questions will allow you to obtain enough information to take a very basic accident report.

To obtain the victim's personal information, refer to "Traffic Stops, Obtaining Information" on page 46 of this book. When you reach the point of obtaining the suspect's personal information (known or unknown suspect) refer to page 41.

The following questions are specifically related to an accident.

¿Quién estaba manejando este carro?
(Who was driving this car?)

OR ### ¿Quién estaba manejando?
(Who was driving?)

¿Qué carro estaba manejando?
(Which vehicle were you driving?)

¿Necesita atención médica?
(Do you need medical attention?)

¿Hay testigos?
(Are there witnesses?)

¿De qué dirección venía?
(Which direction were you coming from?)

¿En cuál carril?
(Which lane?)

¿Su velocidad?
(Your speed?)

¿De dónde venía el otro carro?
(Where did the other car come from?)

¿En cuál carril venía?
(Which lane was it in?)

¿Había pasajeros?

(Were there passengers?)

¿Dónde están?

(Where are they?)

¿De qué color era el semáforo?

(What color was the light?)

	POSSIBLE ANSWERS:		
		Apenas cambió.	(It just changed.)
		Acaba de cambiar.	(It just changed.)
		Verde	(Green)
		Amarillo	(Yellow)
		Rojo	(Red)

¿Estaba usando su cinturón/cinto de seguridad?

(Were you using your belt/seat belt?)

(REFER TO PAGE 46, TRAFFIC, OBTAINING INFORMATION)

STOLEN VEHICLE INVESTIGATIONS

¿Qué clase de carro tiene? ¿Honda, Chevy, Ford?
(What kind of car do you have?)

¿Qué tipo? ¿Carro, camioneta {"van"} camión/troka?
(What type is it? Car, van, truck?)

> **IF TRUCK:** *¿Doble cabina?*
> (Extended cab/double cab?)

¿El año?
(The year?)

¿El color?
(The color?)

¿Cuántas puertas tiene?
(How many doors does it have?)

¿Cuáles son los números o letras de la placa?
(What is the license plate?)

¿De qué estado es la placa?
(From what state is the license plate?)

¿Hay algo único/diferente en el vehículo?
(Is there anything unique about the vehicle?)

¿Dónde estuvo parqueado?
(Where was it parked?)

¿A qué hora salió del vehículo?
(When did you leave the vehicle?)

¿A qué hora regresó?

(What time did you return?)

¿Alguien más tiene llaves del vehículo?

(Does anyone else have keys to the vehicle?)

¿Quién es el dueño registrado?

(Who is the registered owner?)

¿El vehículo está pagado?

(Is the vehicle paid off?)

DRUG INVESTIGATIONS

Miranda Warnings

Usted tiene el derecho de guarder silencio.

Cualquier cosa que diga se puede usar en su contra en los tribunales de justicia.

Usted tiene el derecho de tener un abogado presente antes y durante las preguntas si usted lo desea.

Si usted no tiene los fondos para pagar un abogado, usted tiene el derecho a que el tribunal le nombre a uno para que le asista antes de comenzar con las preguntas.

¿Comprende usted estos derechos?   *¿Sí o no?*

OPTIONS: Ask the subject if they can read: *¿Puede leer?*

If YES, you can hand them the Miranda warnings and have the subject read the warnings: *Léalo, por favor.*

Make sure you ask them if they understood their rights: *¿Comprende usted estos derechos?*   *¿Sí o no?*

BE CAUTIOUS of having them read their own rights, many of the Spanish speakers law enforcement comes into contact with will not know how to read or write, yet may not admit this fact.

Types Of Drugs

Coca, Perico, Blanco, Nieve, Polvo, La Huera, Blanco	Cocaine
Negro, Chiva, Cargada, Llanta, Pedazo (5 g.)	Heroin
Mota, Marijuana	Marijuana
Piedra	Crack cocaine
Crystal, Meta, "G", Vidrio, Hielo, Ventana	Methamphetamine

Possession Cases – On Foot

¿Puedo hablar con usted?
(Can I talk to you?)

¿Usted tiene alguna drogas en su persona?
(Do you have any drugs on you?)

¿Le puedo registrar? OR **¿Le puedo esculcar?**
(Can I search you?)

¿Le puedo registrar para drogas o armas? OR
¿Le puedo esculcar para drogas o armas?
(Can I search you for drugs or weapons?)

¿Usted tiene cualquier cosa afilada en sus bolsillos?
(Do you have anything sharp in your pockets?)

¿Qué tipo de drogas son éstas?
(What type of drugs is this?)

¿Las drogas son suyas?
(Are the drugs yours?)

¿Dónde las consiguió?
(Where did you get it?)

¿Cuánto pagó por las drogas?
(How much did you pay for the drugs?)

¿Ésta es su camisa? OR **¿Es su camisa?** OR **¿Su camisa?**
(Is this your shirt?)

¿Son sus pantalones?
(Are these your pants?)

¿Son sus calcetines?
(Are these your socks?)

¿Son sus zapatos?
(Are these your shoes?)

¿Es su sombrero? OR **¿Es su cachucha/gorra?**
(Is this your hat? OR Is this your baseball hat?)

Possession Cases – In Vehicles

¿Es su vehículo? OR **¿Es su carro?**
(Is this your vehicle? OR Is this your car?)

¿Alguien más maneja el vehículo/el carro?
(Does anyone else drive the vehicle/the car?)
> **¿Quién?**
> (Who?)

¿A quién le pertenece el vehículo/el carro? OR **¿Quién es el dueño?**
(Who does the vehicle/car belong to?)
> **Amigo**
> (Friend)
> **Pariente**
> (Relative)
> **Novia**
> (Girlfriend)
> **Novio**
> (Boyfriend)

¿Cómo se llama él/ella?
(What is his/her name?)

¿Cuánto tiempo ha manejado el vehículo/el carro?
(How long have you been driving the vehicle/the car?)

> ***¿Días?***
> (Days)
>
> ***¿Semanas?***
> (Weeks)
>
> ***¿Meses?***
> (Months)

¿A qué hora empezó a manejar el vehículo/el carro hoy? OR
¿A qué hora empezó a manejar el vehículo/el carro esta noche?
(What time did you start driving the vehicle today/tonight?)

¿Puedo revisar el vehículo/el carro?
(Can I search the vehicle/the car?)

¿Puedo revisar el vehículo/el carro por drogas o armas?
(Can I search the vehicle/car for drugs or weapons?)

¿Sabía usted que las drogas estaban adentro del vehículo/carro?
(Did you know the drugs were in the vehicle/car?)

¿Estaran sus huellas digitales en las bolsas?
(Will your fingerprints be on the bags?)

Possession For Sale

¿Vende drogas?
(Do you sell drugs?)

¿Qué tipo(s)?
(What type/s?)

¿Dónde consigue las drogas?
(Where do you get your drugs?)

¿Qué tipo de drogas vende él/ella?
(What type of drugs does he/she sell?)

¿Cómo se llama la persona que le vendió las drogas?
(From who do you buy your drugs?)

¿Cómo se pone en contacto con él/ella?
(How do you contact him/her?)

¿Número de teléfono?
(Phone number?)

¿Qué tipo de carro maneja él/ella?
(What type of vehicle does he/she drive?)
    ¿Color?
    (Color?)

¿Dónde vive él/ella?
(Where does he/she live?)

¿Cuánto gana cada día?
(How much do you make a day?)

¿Cuánto gana cada semana?
(How much do you make a week?)

¿Tiene otras formas de ingresos?
(Do you have any other source of income?)

Possession Cases – Houses/apartments

¿Esta es su casa?
(Is this your house?)

¿Cuánto tiempo ha vivido en esta casa o apartamento?
(How long have you lived here, in this house/apartment?)
¿Quién mas vive aqui?
(Who else lives here?)

¿Paga renta?
(Do you pay rent?)

¿Quién mas tiene las llaves de su casa/apartamento?
(Does anyone else have keys to the house/apartment?)

¿Nombre?
(Name?)

¿Hay drogas adentro de la casa?
(Are there any drugs in the house?)

¿Hay armas adentro de la casa?
(Are there any weapons in the house?)

¿Podemos revisar su casa por drogas o armas? OR
¿Podemos buscar si hay drogas o armas en su casa?
(Can we search the house for drugs or weapons? OR Can we look to see if there are any drugs or weapons in your house?)

Miscellaneous Expressions/questions

Hablo poco español.
(I speak only a little Spanish.)

Hable despacio por favor.
(Please speak slowly.)

Repita por favor.
(Repeat please.)

No entiendo.
(I do not understand.)

¿Esta es su recámara/su cuarto?
(Is this your bedroom/room?)

¿Duerme aquí?
(Do you sleep here?)

¿Dónde estan las drogas?
(Where are the drugs?)

ALCOHOL INFLUENCE REPORT

In this section are some open-ended questions. Be cautious of asking open-ended questions since you may not understand the response. Consider asking only the closed-ended so that you will better understand the answer.

¿Estaba manejando el vehículo? ¿Sí o no?
(Were you operating the vehicle? Yes or no?)

¿Para dónde iba?
(Where were you going?)

¿De dónde empezó?
(From where did you start?)

¿A qué hora se fue?
(At what time did you leave?)

¿Qué hora es ahora?
(What time is it now?)

¿Cuál es la fecha de hoy?
(What is the date today?)

¿Cuál es la día de la semana hoy?
(What day of the week is it?)

¿Qué ha estado tomando?
(What have you been drinking?)

¿Cuánto ha tomado?
(How much did you drink?)

¿Adónde estaba tomando?
(Where were you drinking?)

¿A qué hora empezó a tomar?
(What time did you start drinking?)

¿A qué hora paró de tomar?
(What time did you stop drinking?)

¿Tuvo un accidente? ¿Sí o no?
(Did you have an accident? Yes or no?)

     IF YES: ***¿Adónde?***
                (Where?)

          ¿A qué hora ocurrió el accidente?
          (What time did the accident occur?)

          ¿Ha tomado despues del accidente? ¿Sí o no?
          (Have you been drinking since the accident?
          Yes or no?)

     IF YES: ***¿Qué ha tomado y cuánto?***
                (What and how much?)

¿Adónde fue cuando la policía lo paró?
(At what location were you stopped?)

¿Está golpeado? ¿Sí o no?
(Are you hurt? Yes or no?)

     IF YES: ***¿Adónde está golpeado?***
                (Where?)

¿Recibió un inchazón en la cabeza?
(Did you get a bump on the head?)

     IF YES: ***¿Cómo ocurrió el golpe en la cabeza.?***
                (Describe how the injury occurred?)

¿Está enfermo?

(Are you ill?)

      IF YES: *Describa su enfermedad.*

                  (Describe illness.)

¿Ha visto a un médico o dentista en las últimas dos semanas?
¿Sí o no?

(Have you been to a doctor or dentist in the last two weeks? Yes or no?)

      IF YES: *¿Cuándo?*

                  (When?)

                  ¿Cuál fue la razón de su visita?

                  (What was the reason for the visit?)

¿De qué se trata los tratamientos? OR *¿Cómo son los tratamientos?*

(Nature of ongoing treatment?)

¿Ha tomado algún medicamento en las últimas veinticuatro horas?

(Have you taken any medication in the past twenty four hours?)

      IF YES: *¿La fecha cuando lo tomó?*

                  (The date taken?)

                  ¿A qué hora se lo tomó?

                  (Time taken?)

                  ¿Tipo de medicamento? ¿Nombre?

                  (Type of medication?)

¿Usted tiene diabetes? ¿Sí o no?

(Do you have diabetes?)

¿Usted toma insulina?

(Do you take insulin for any reason?)

      IF YES: *¿Por qué?*

                  (Why?)

¿Usted tiene alergias?
(Do you have any allergies?)
> **IFYES:** ***¿Cuáles son?***
>
> (What are they?)

¿Le molestan sus alergias ahora?
(Are your allergies bothering you now?)

¿Usted tiene alguna discapacidad física?
(Do you have any physical disabilities?)
> **IF YES:** ***Describa.***
>
> (Describe.)

¿Se encuentra el oficial que lo arrestó en este momento?
(Is the officer that arrested you here now?)

¿Cuándo comió por última vez?
(When did you last eat?)

¿Que fué lo que comió?
(What did you eat?)

¿Qué tanto ha dormido en las últimas veinticuatro horas?
(How much sleep have you had in the last twenty four hours?)

¿A qué hora se levantó hoy?
(When did you wake up today?)

¿Usted pudo sentir los efectos del alcohol mientras manejaba el vehículo?
(Could you feel the effects of the alcohol in any way while you were driving?)

***Usando una escala de cero a diez, cero siendo completamente sano y
diez completamente borracho, ¿cómo usted se mide durante el tiempo
que estaba manejando el vehículo?***

(On scale of 0 to 10, 0 being completely sober and ten being completely
drunk, how would you rate yourself at the time you were driving?)

***¿Ha sido arrestado anteriormente por manejar un vehículo baja la
influéncia de alcohol?***

(Do you have any prior DUI convictions?)